I0467397

Copyright © 2015 Creative Christmas Coloring

All Rights Reserved Worldwide

CREATIVE & FESTIVE
Christmas Coloring Book

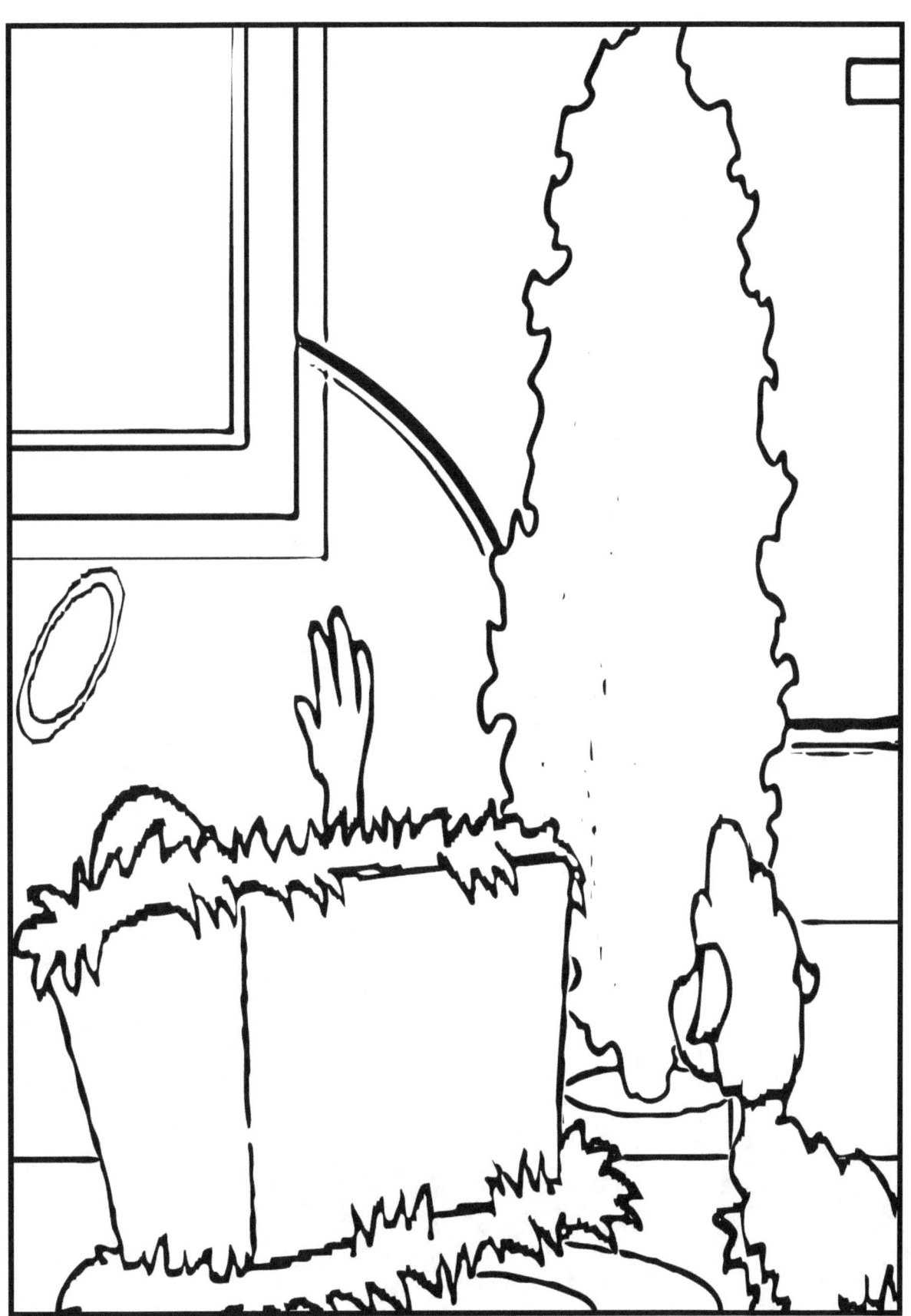

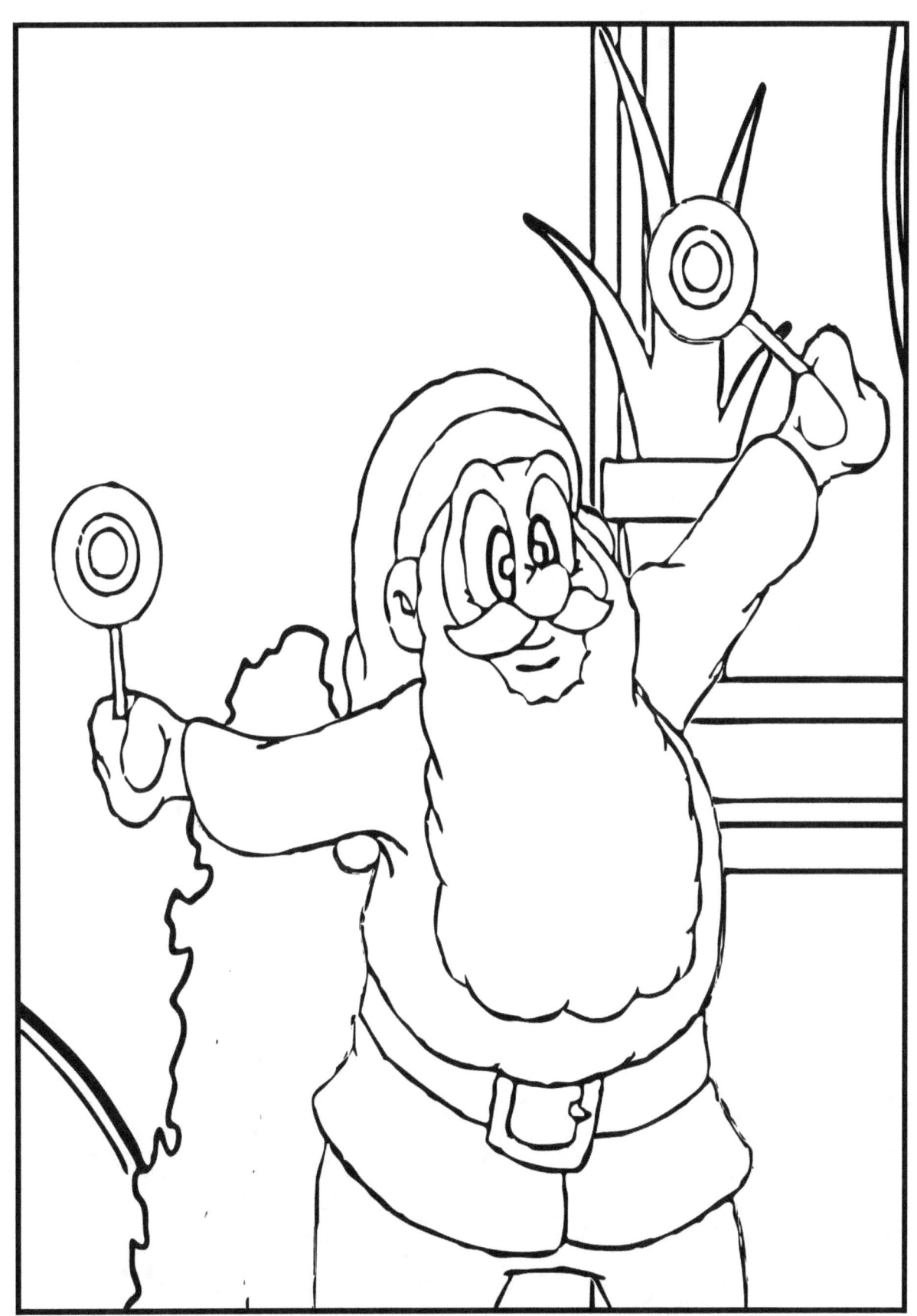

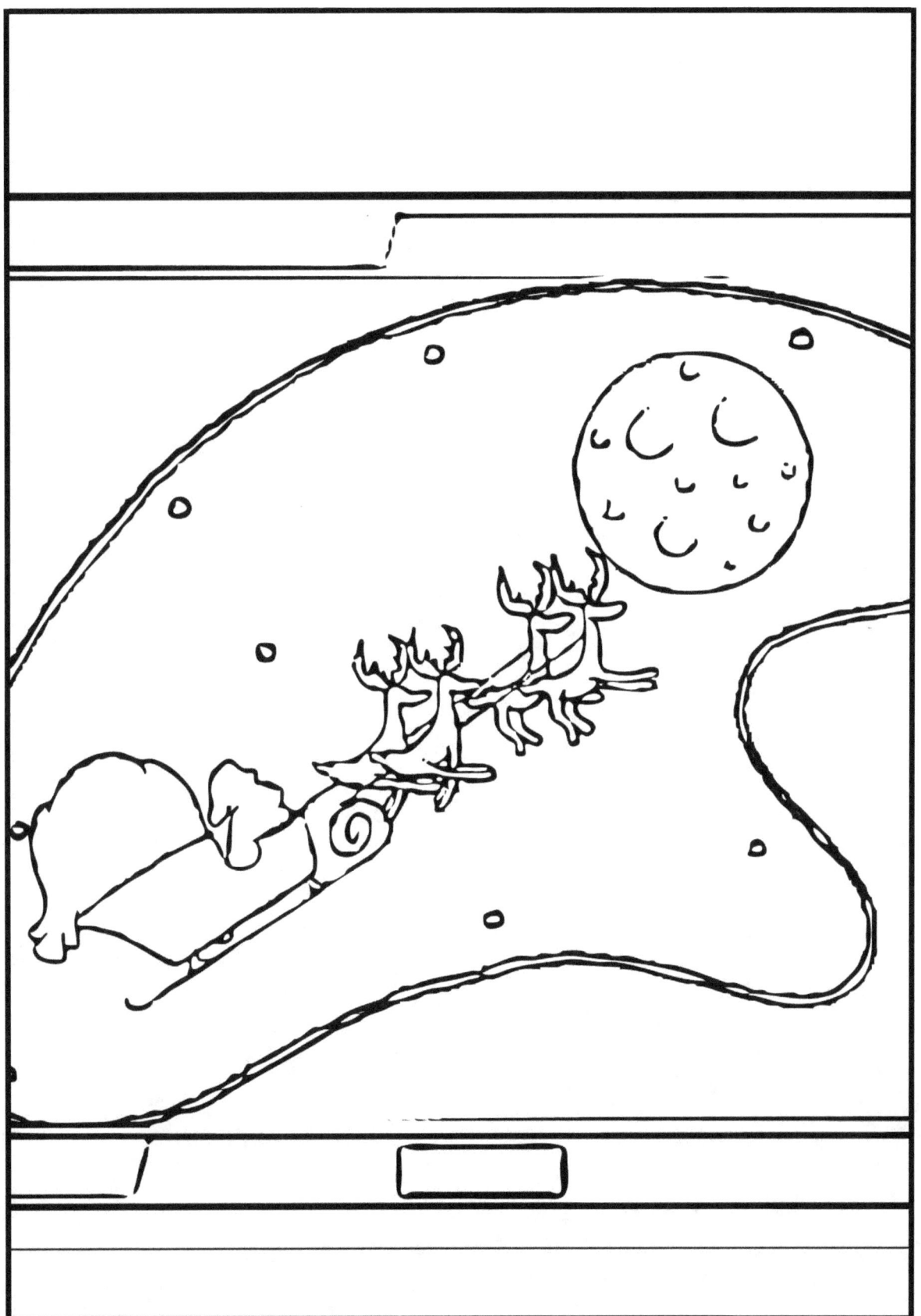

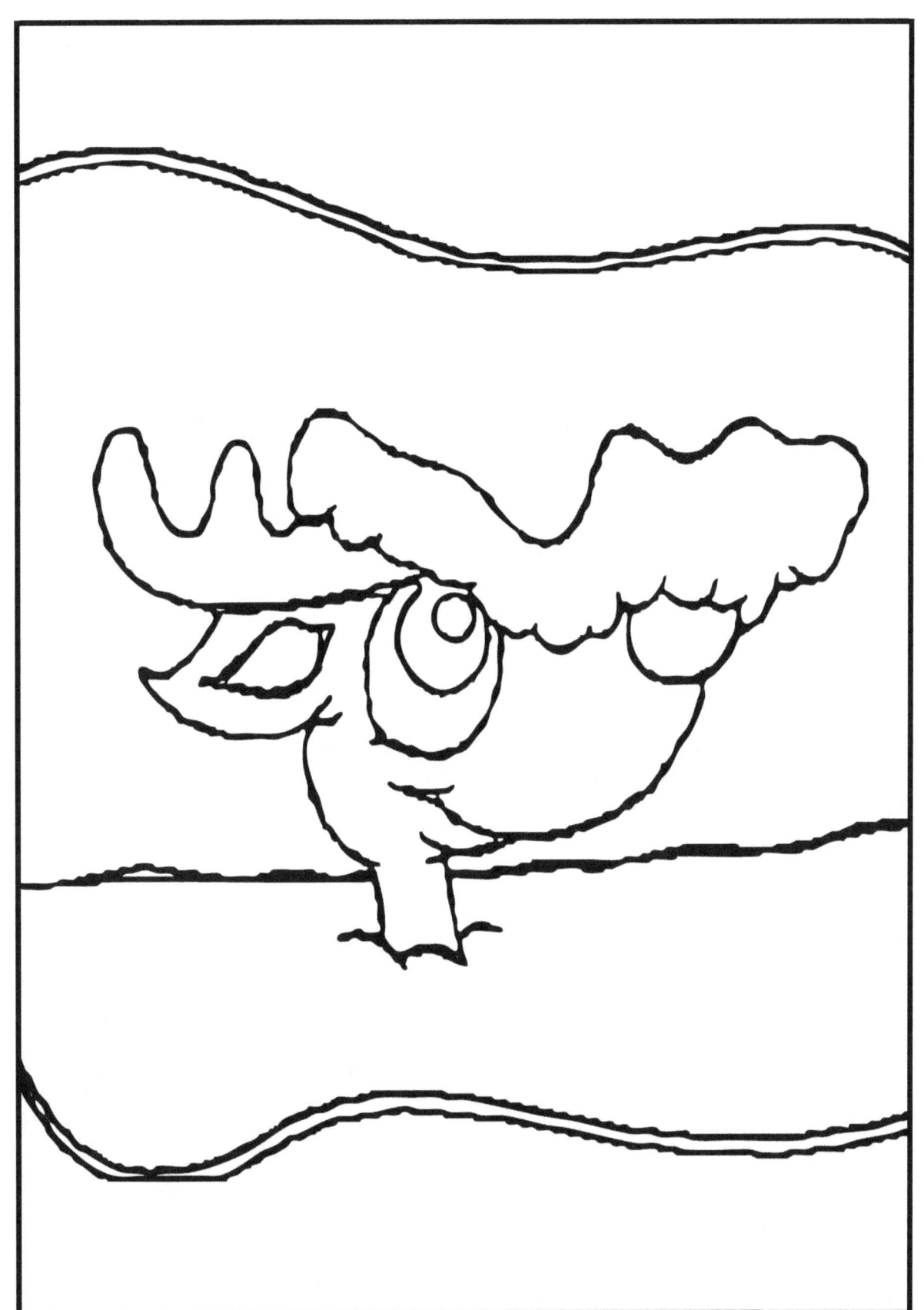

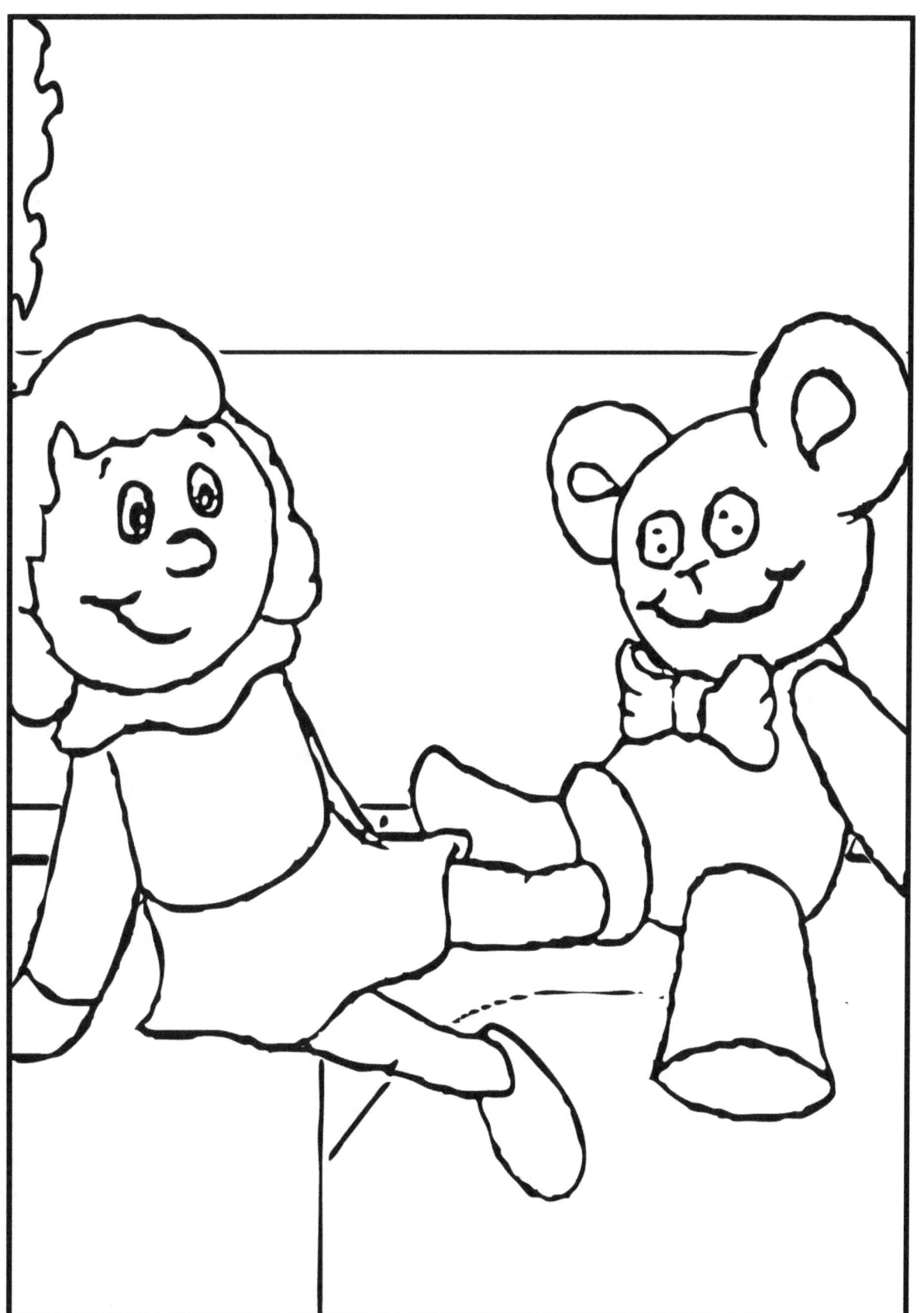

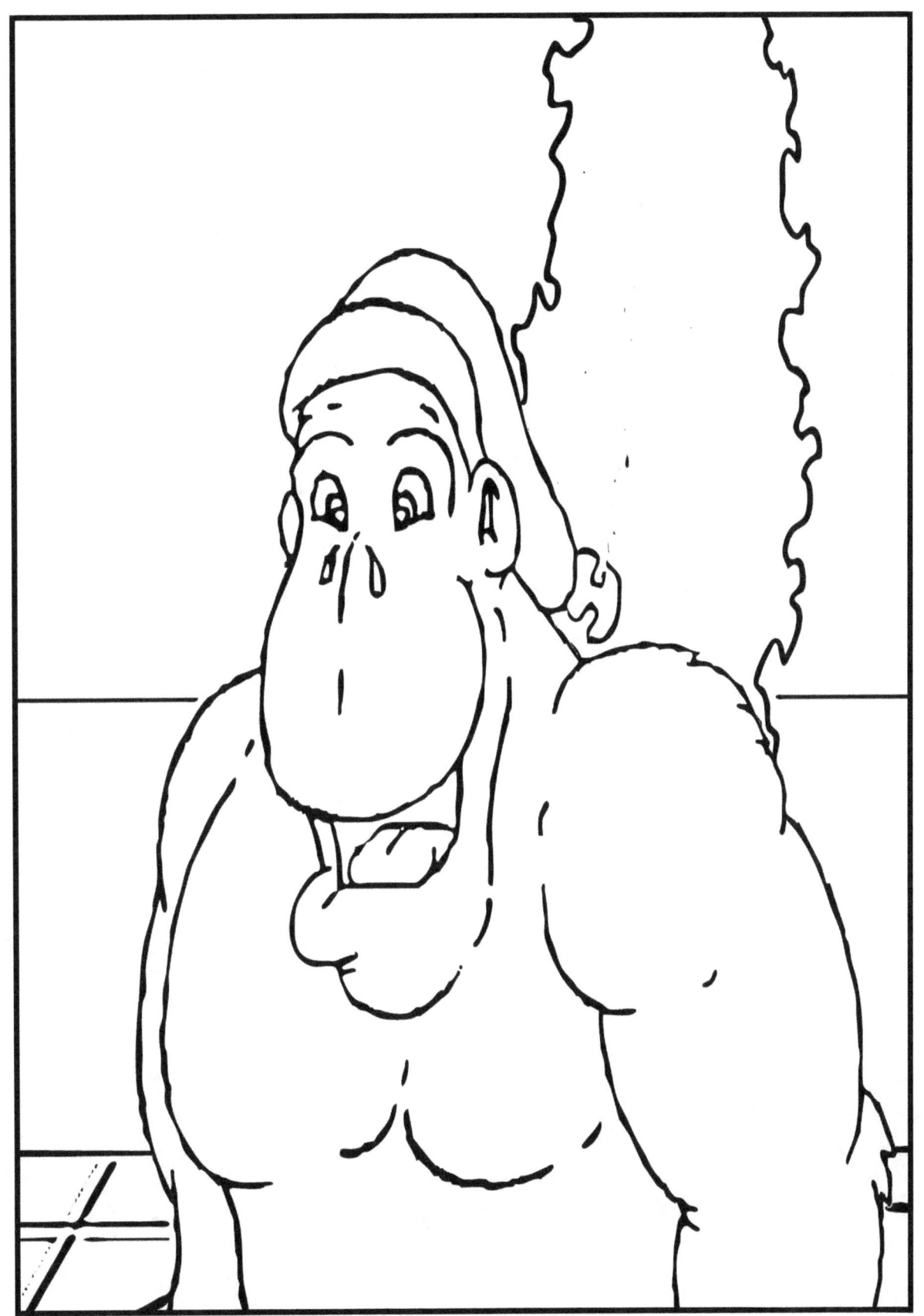

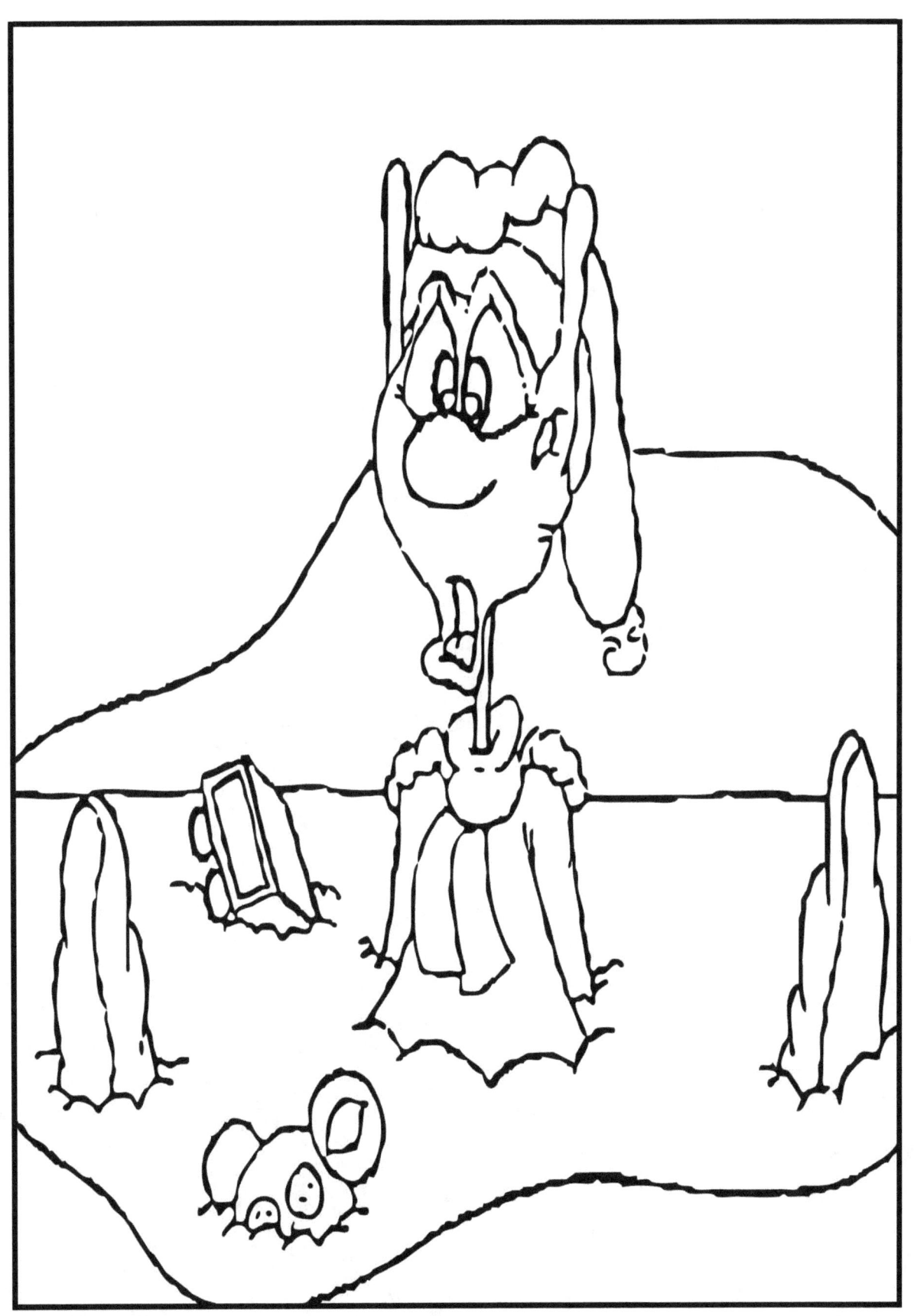

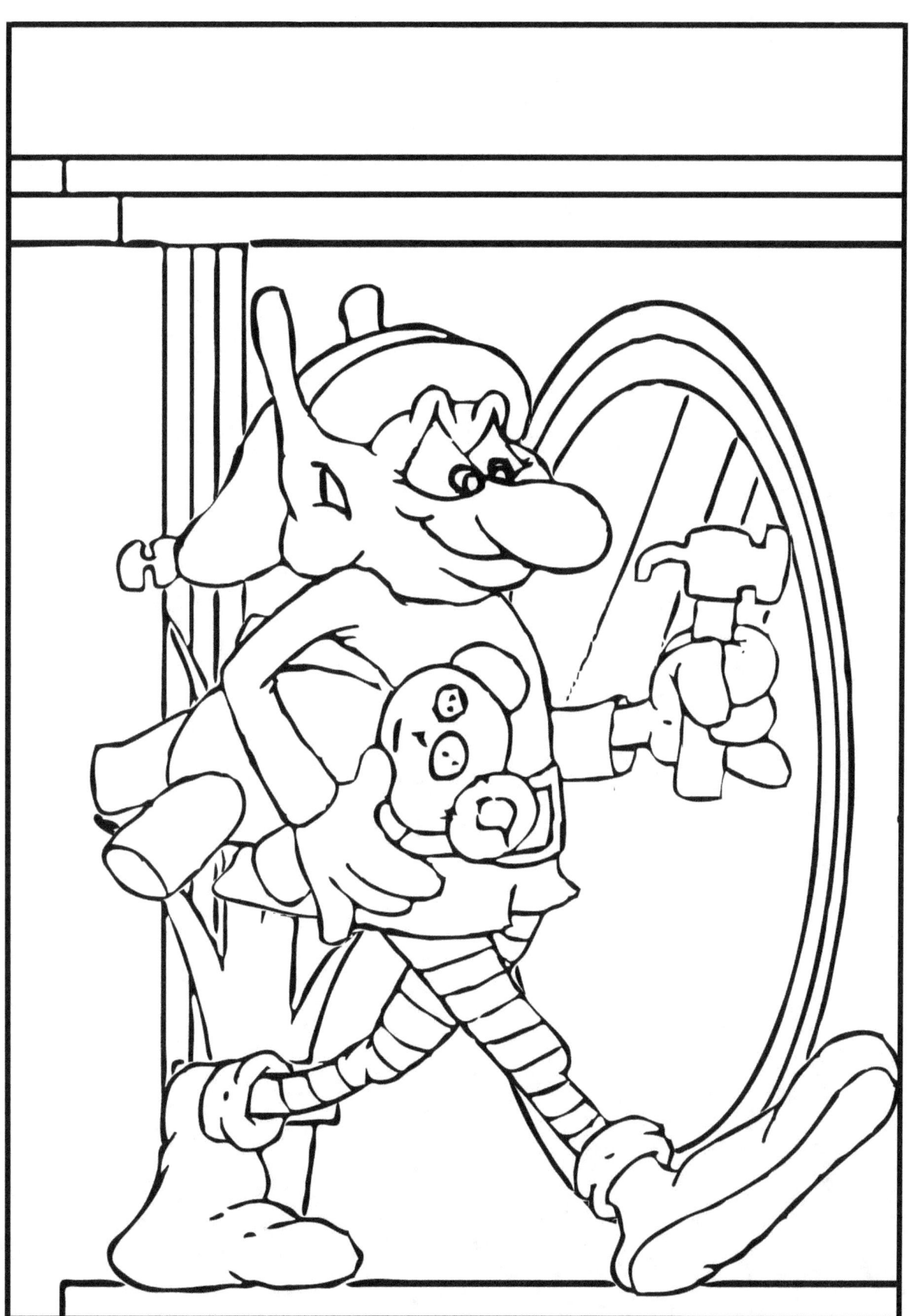

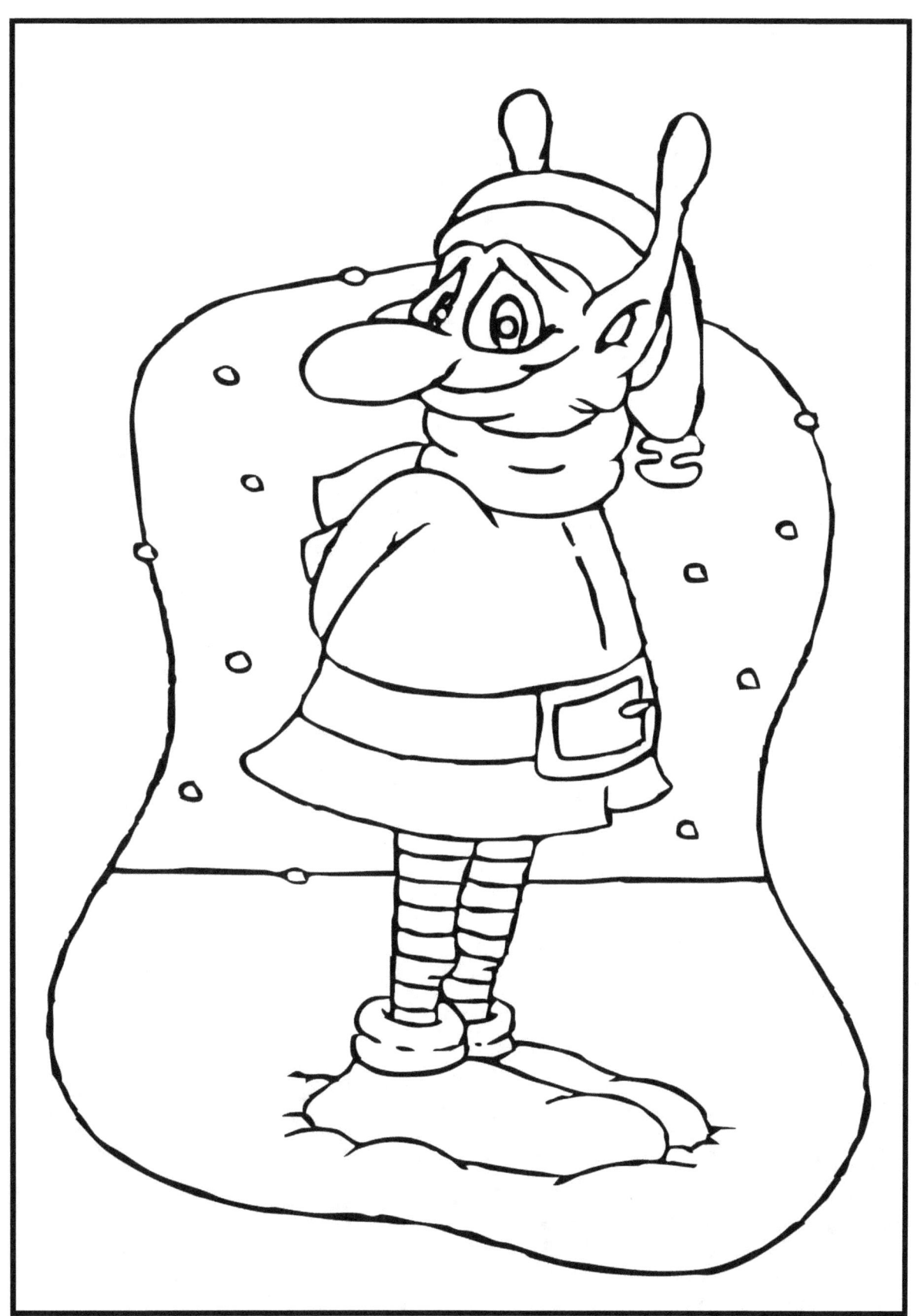

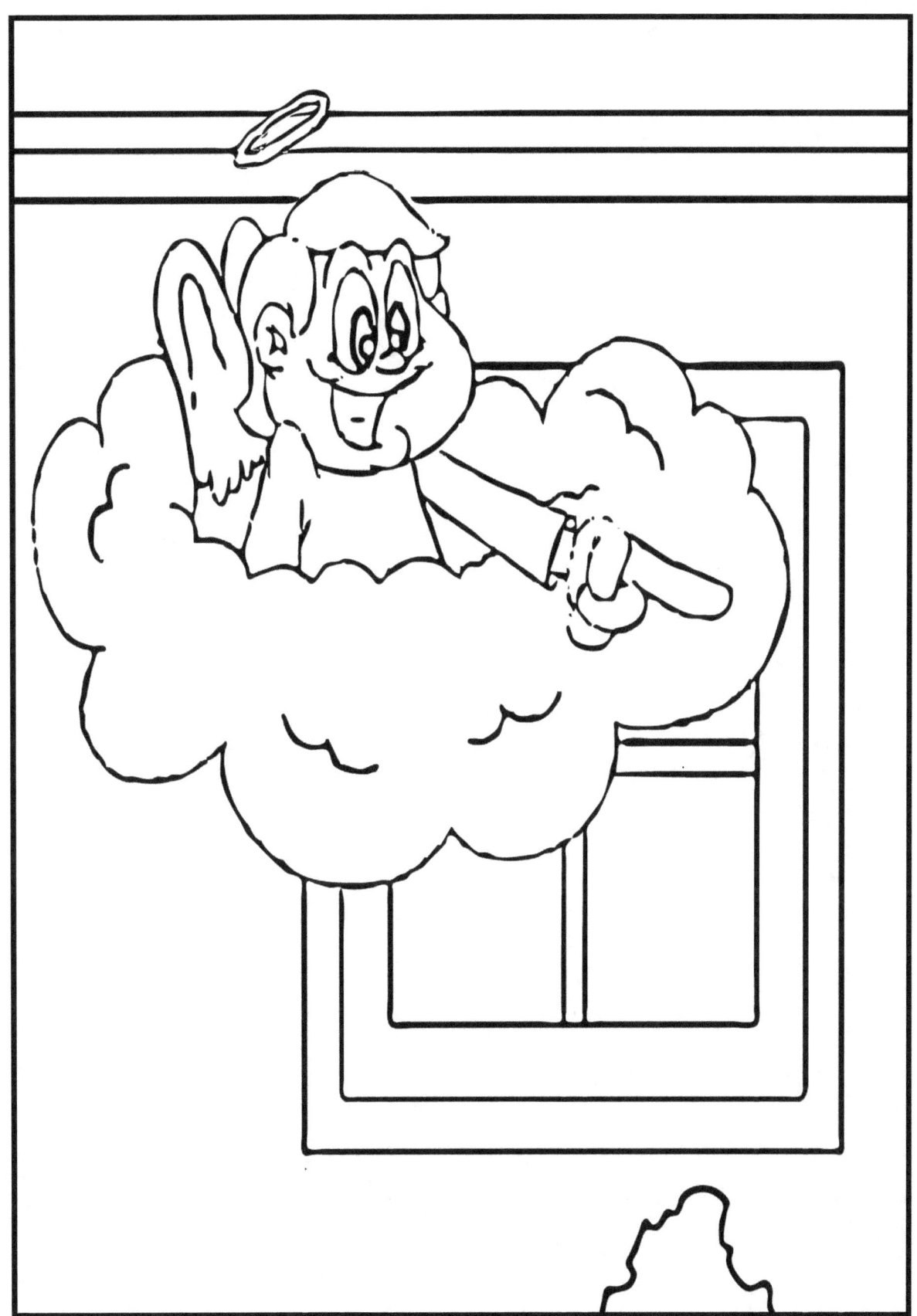

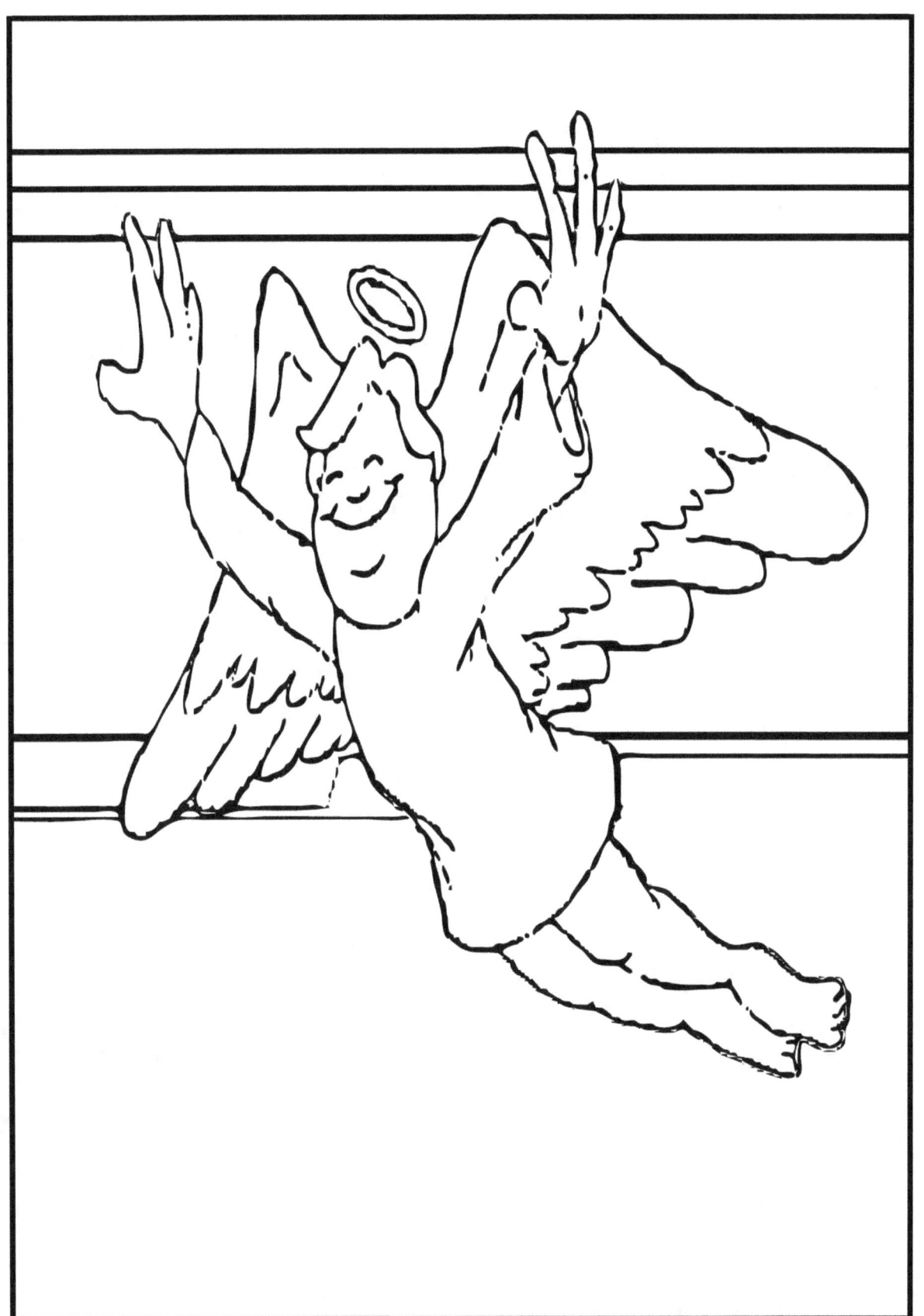

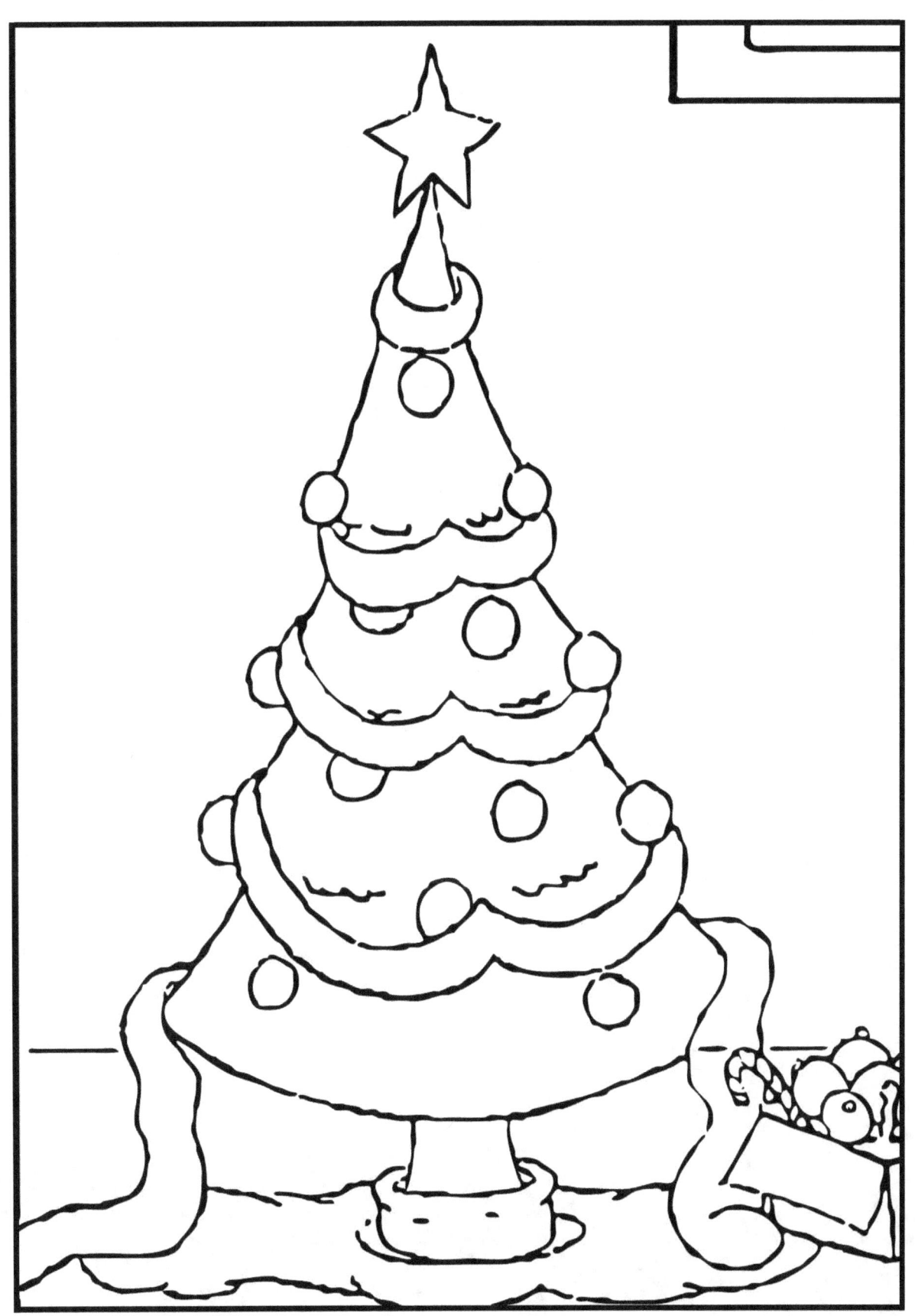

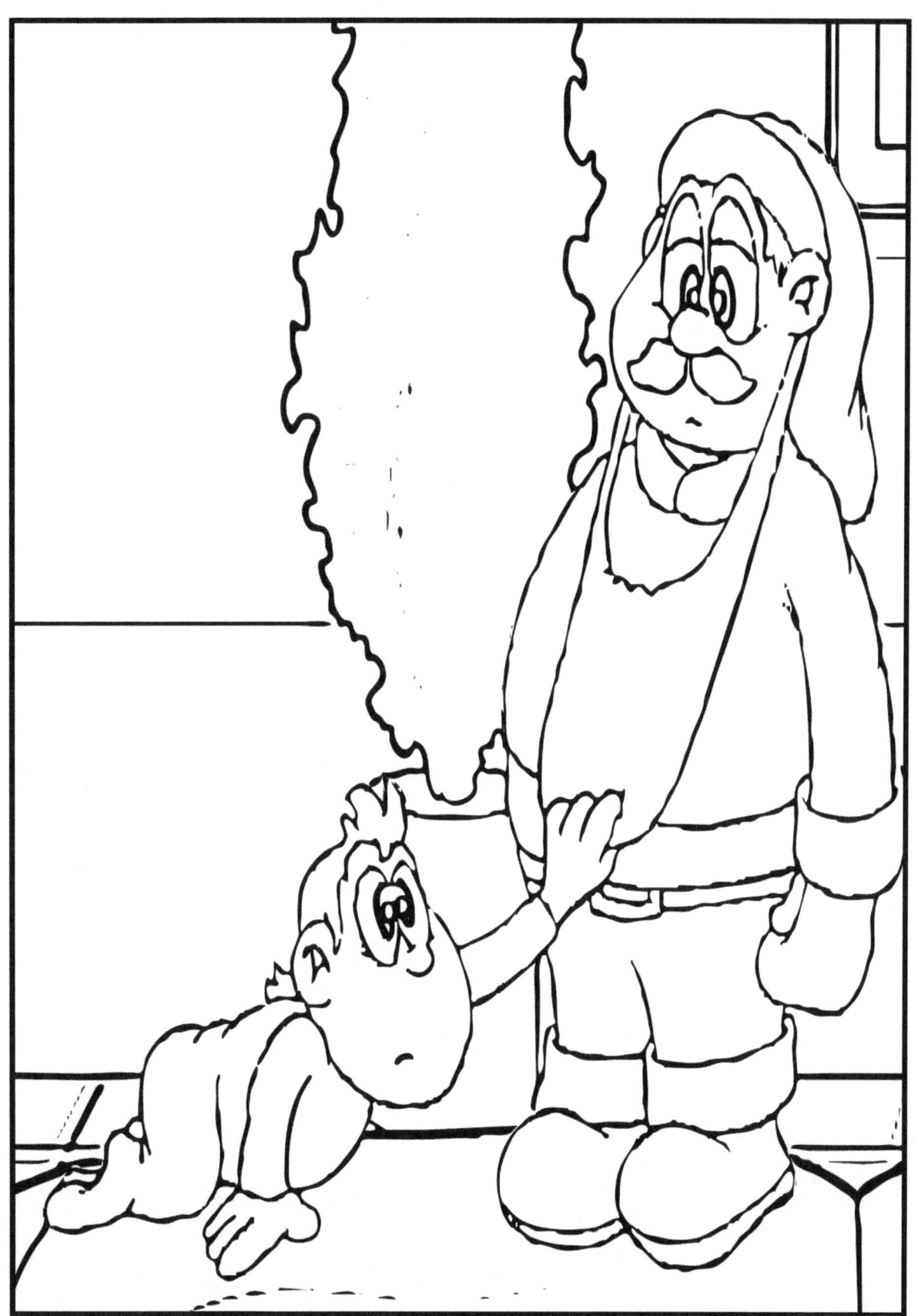

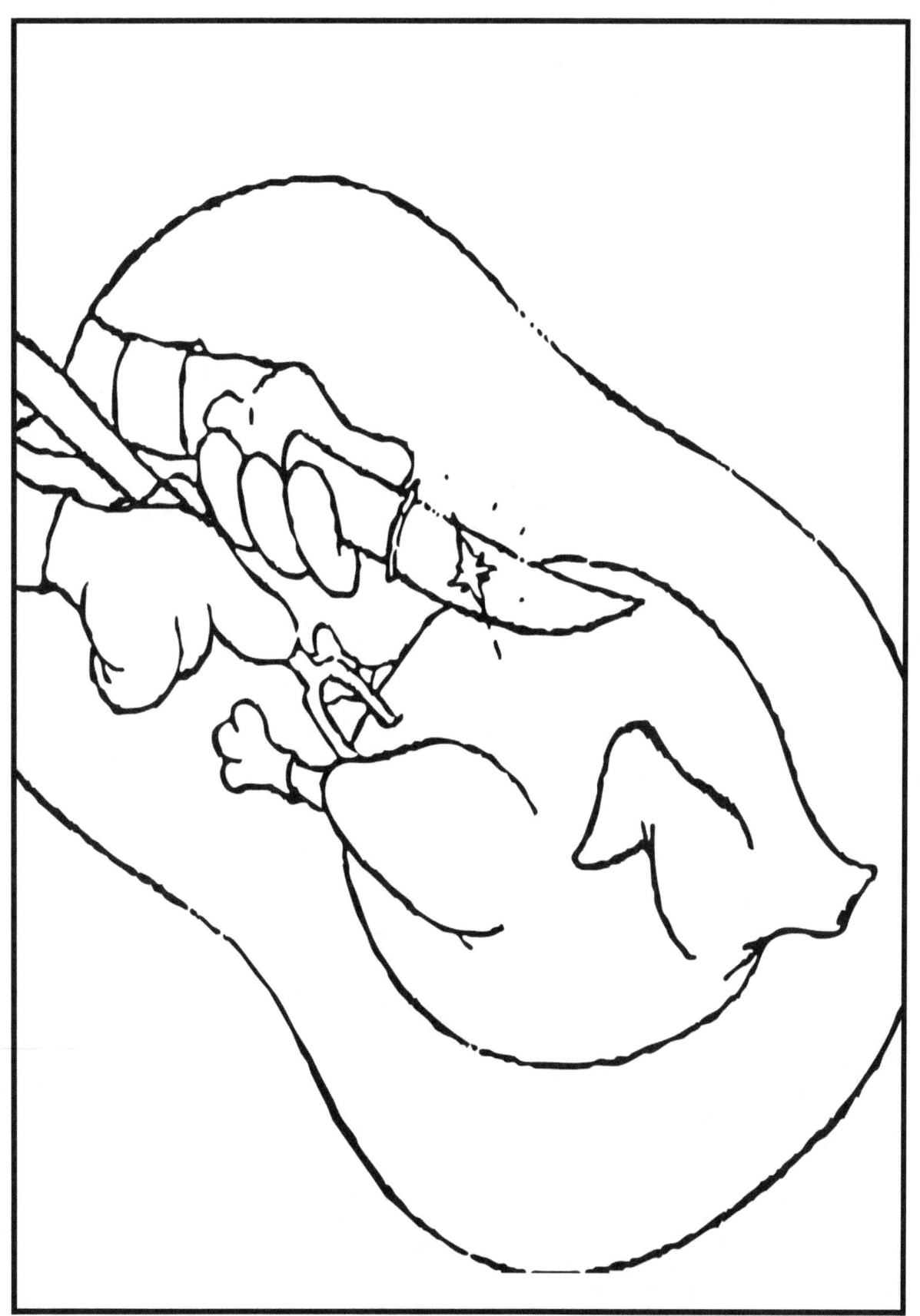

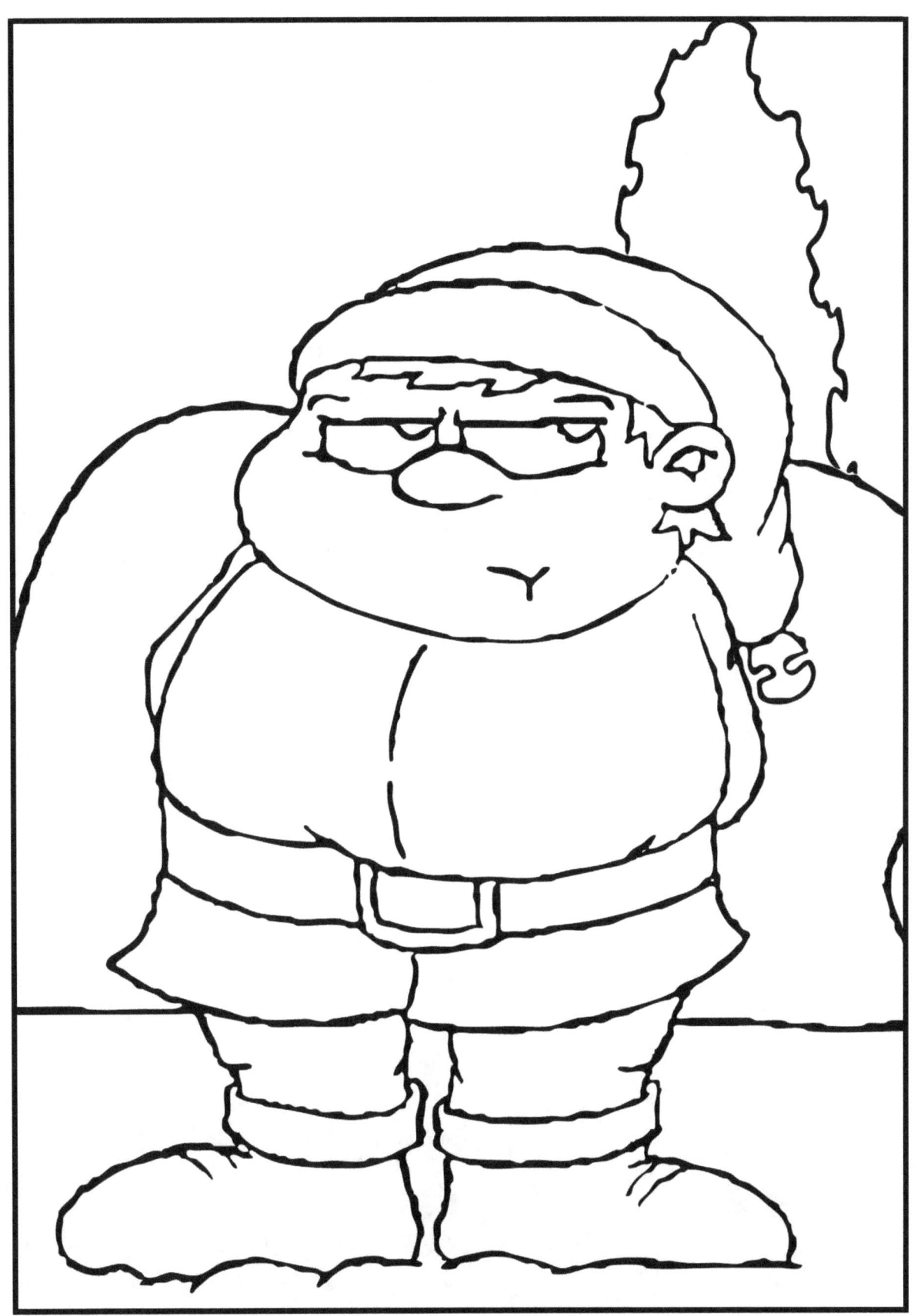

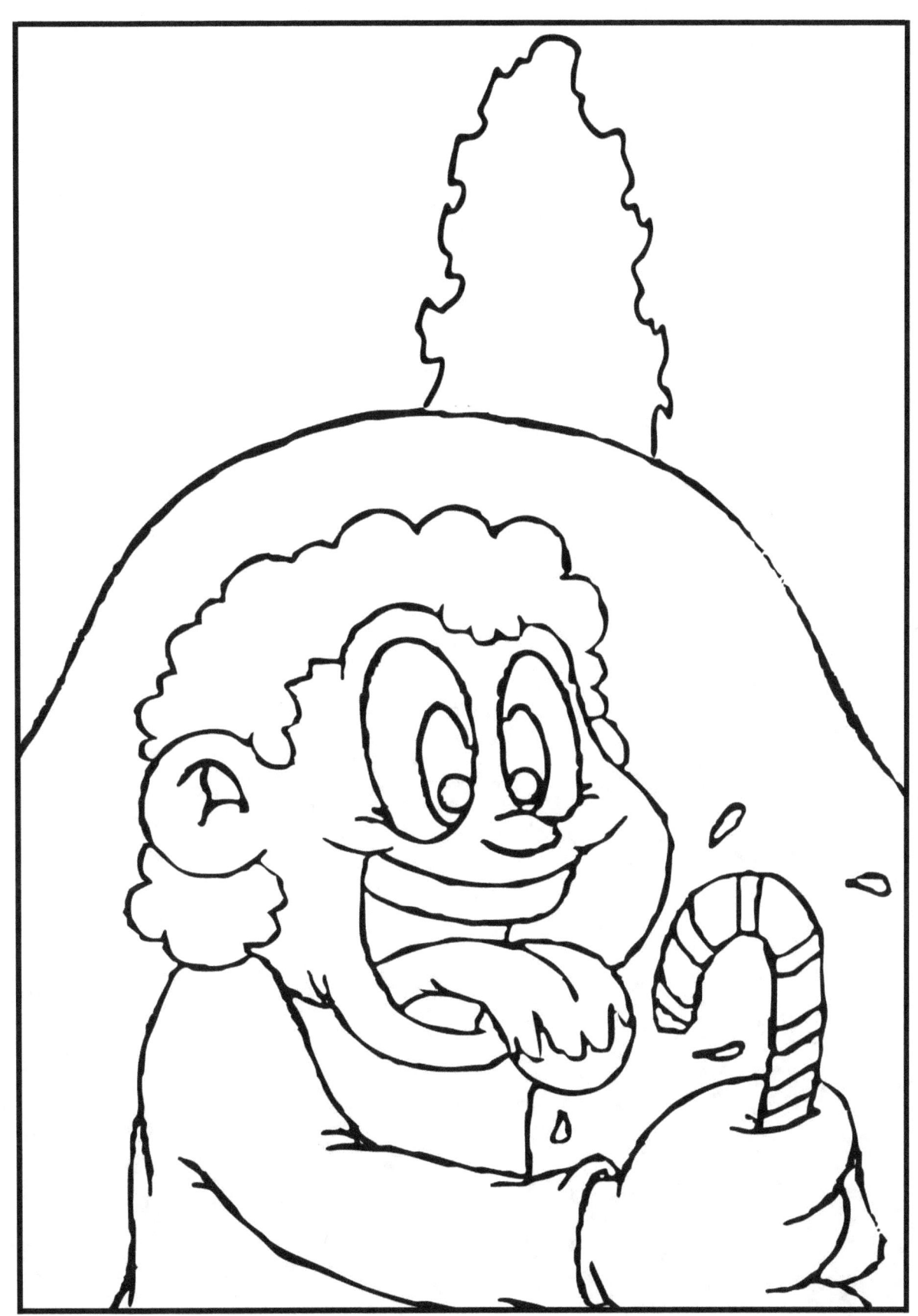

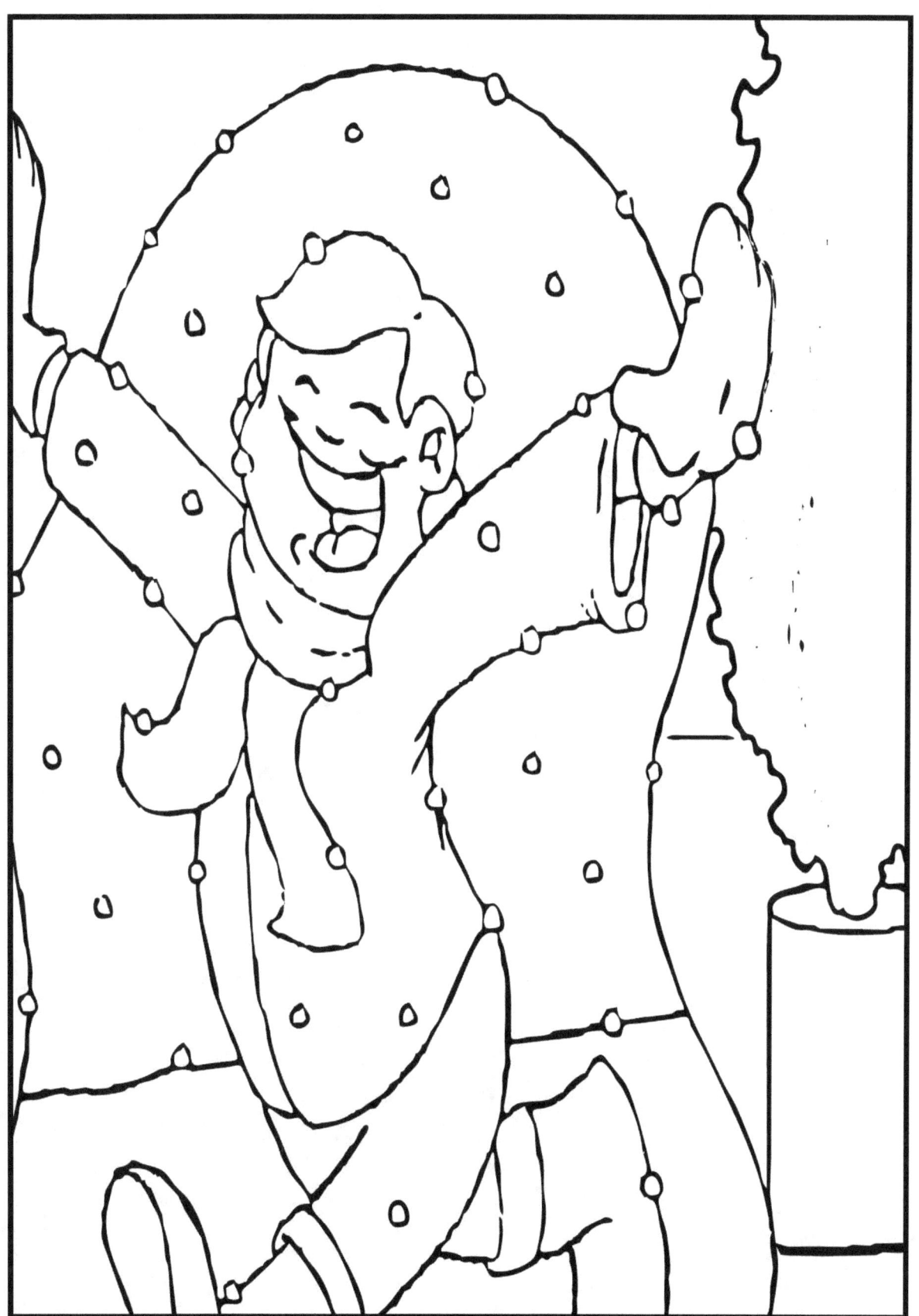

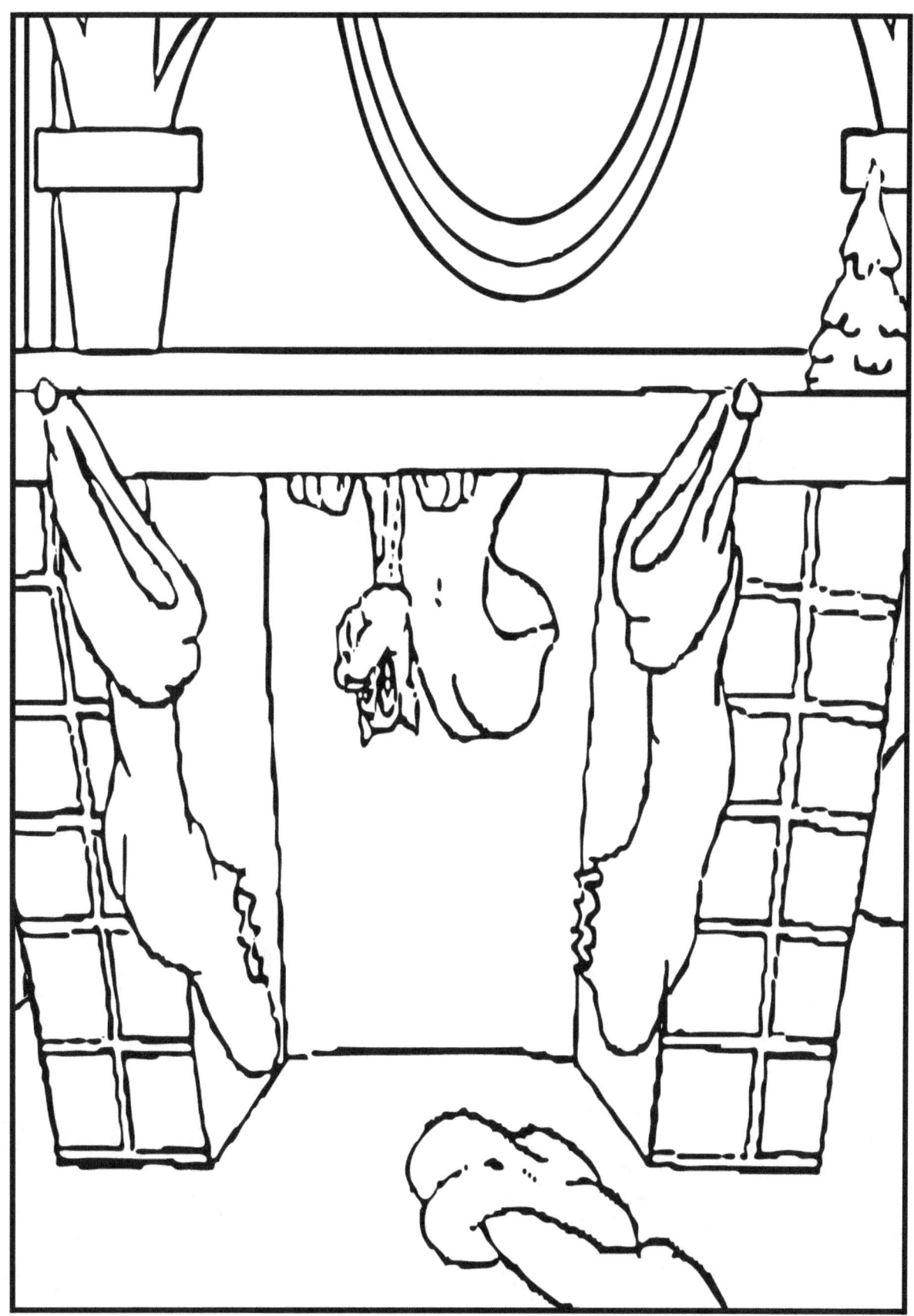

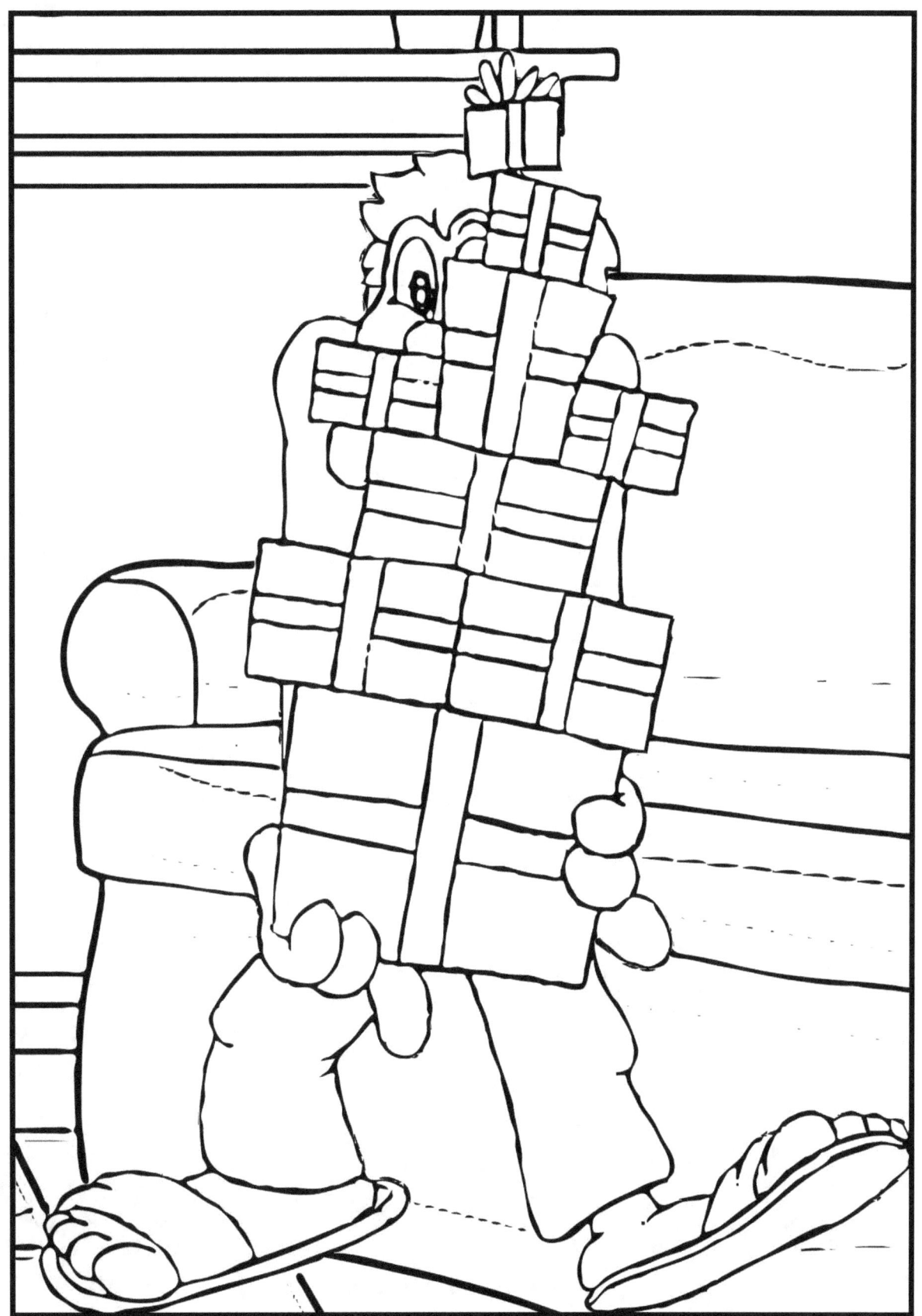

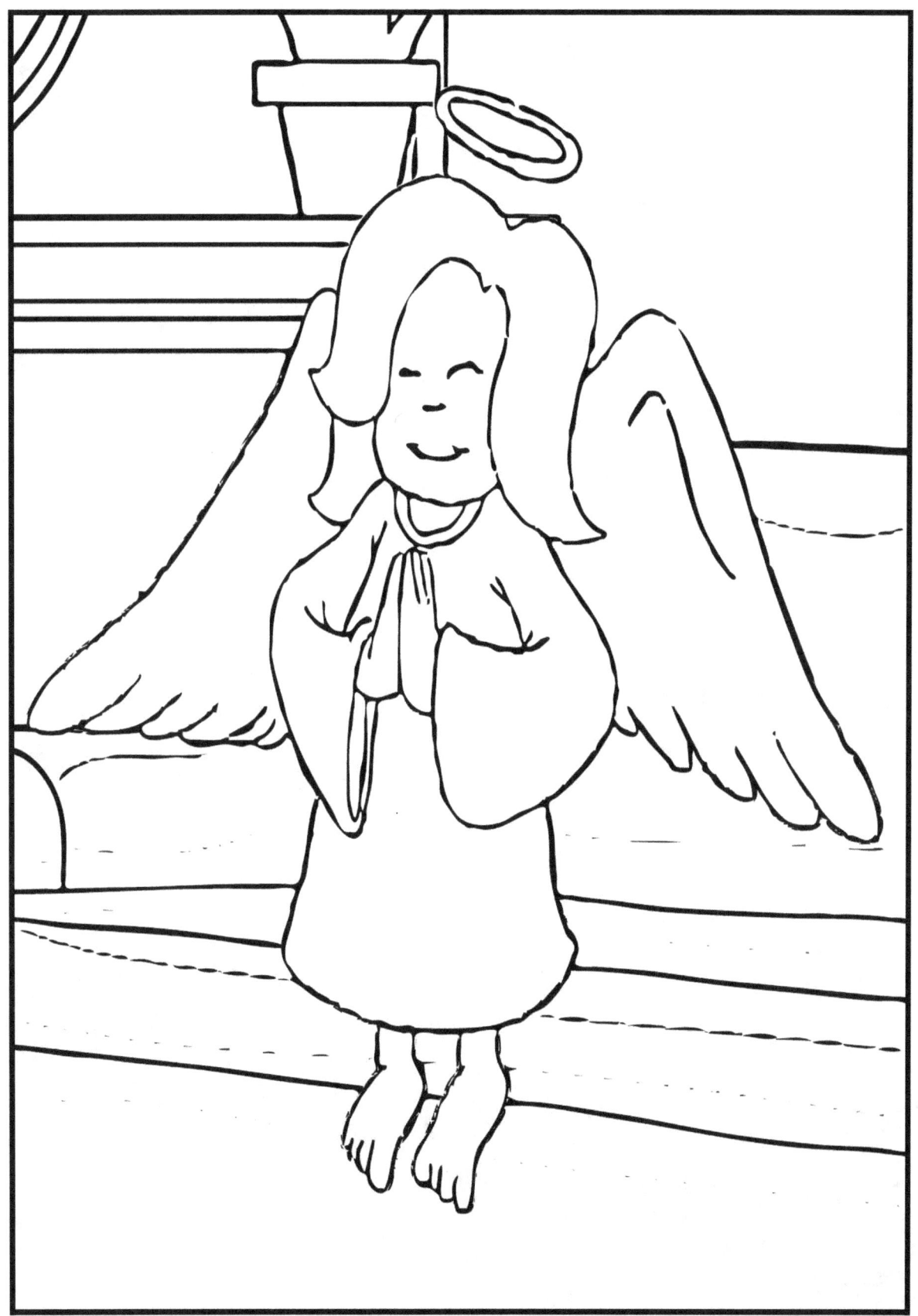

www.ingramcontent.com/pod-product-compliance
Lightning Source LLC
Chambersburg PA
CBHW081401170526
45166CB00010B/3161